Climb Any Mountain

Name _____

Mountains are many different shapes and sizes. Build a puzzle with the names of some of the most famous mountains on earth. **Hint:** Build off Aconcagua first.

Word Box

Cook	Cotopaxi	Hood	Kenya
Logan	Longs (Peak)	Everest	Ararat
Kilimanjaro	Lassen (Peak)	Makalu	Shasta
Cayambe	Pikes (Peak)	Whitney	Fugi
Annapurna	Matterhorn	Erebus	

Palindromes – Wow!

Name _____

A palindrome is a word that reads the same backward and forward. Use the words in the Word Box to complete the sentences.

Word Box			
bob	deed	civic	level
nun	peep	radar	refer
ewe	kayak	redder	solos

1. It is your _____ duty to vote in the election.

2. Please _____ to your dictionary for the correct spelling of that word.

3. The longer I stay in the sun, the _____ I get.

4. Don't you dare let me hear a _____ out of you.

5. Do you like to _____ for apples on Halloween?

6. The _____ , an Eskimo canoe, is made of skins on a wooden frame.

7. The _____ and the ram have woolly coats.

8. Gino was awarded a medal for his brave _____ .

9. My sister is a _____ and teaches elementary school.

10. Do you see the plane on the _____ screen?

11. Have you sung many _____ before?

12. The land was _____ for as far as one could see.

Think of three palindromes of your own and write a sentence for each one.

_____

_____

_____

_____

Code Names

Name _____

Use the code to write a synonym for each word.

a	c	e	i	m	n	o	p	q	r	s	t	u	v	x	y	z
1	2	3	4	5	6	7	8	9	10	11	12	13	14	15	16	17

1. surprise – __ __ __ __ __
   1 5 1 17 3

2. anticipate – __ __ __ __ __ __
   3 15 8 3 2 12

3. concern – __ __ __ __ __ __ __
   1 6 15 4 3 12 16

4. forgive – __ __ __ __ __ __
   3 15 2 13 11 3

5. screwy – __ __ __ __ __ __
   4 6 11 1 6 3

6. tempt – __ __ __ __ __ __
   3 6 12 4 2 3

7. expect – __ __ __ __ __ __
   1 11 11 13 5 3

8. thorough –
   __ __ __ __ __ __ __ __ __
   4 6 12 3 6 11 4 14 3

9. eat – __ __ __ __ __ __ __
   2 7 6 11 13 5 3

10. cross –
    __ __ __ __ __ __ __ __ __
    4 6 12 3 10 11 3 2 12

11. slight – __ __ __ __ __
    8 3 12 12 16

12. inactive – __ __ __ __ __ __ __
    8 1 11 11 4 14 3

13. match – __ __ __ __ __ __
    3 9 13 1 12 3

14. sorry – __ __ __ __ __ __ __ __
    8 3 6 4 12 3 6 12

15. rude – __ __ __ __ __
    11 1 11 11 16

16. fragrance – __ __ __ __ __
    11 2 3 6 12

17. delicate –
    __ __ __ __ __ __ __ __ __
    11 3 6 11 4 12 4 14 3

18. truthful –
    __ __ __ __ __ __ __ __ __
    14 3 10 1 2 4 7 13 11

19. impatient – __ __ __ __ __
    12 3 11 12 16

20. follow – __ __ __ __ __
    3 6 11 13 3

Using the same code given at the top of the page, write five more words and the code numbers for their synonyms. Trade papers with a classmate and decipher each other's code words.

Example: penny – __ __ __ __
2 3 6 12

1. _____   4. _____

2. _____   5. _____

3. _____

Scrambled Words

Name _____

Unscramble the letters in parentheses to spell a word that makes sense in each sentence. Write the word in the blank.

1. I like the _____ of that tile floor.
   (n a p t e t r)

2. Troy is so thin he looks like a _____ .
   (k l e o n t e s)

3. Don't be so _____ – say you'll go with us.
   (b u s t o b n r)

4. I was born in the twentieth _____ .
   (y u r n e c t)

5. A good _____ can solve the case.
   (e c t t e v i d e)

6. The police _____ the laws of the land.
   (c e r o n e f)

7. Your favorite program is not on this _____ .
   (n e l n a h c)

8. You will need a _____ because it is very cold tonight.
   (a k n b e l t)

9. Did an _____ of yours come on the *Mayflower*?
   (c e s n t a r o)

10. Did a nail _____ your bike tire?
    (c u t u r p e n)

11. How many people does this football _____ hold?
    (t u m d i s a)

12. I didn't _____ that it was your birthday yesterday.
    (z e l a r e i)

13. All people need food, clothing, and _____ .
    (t e e s h l r)

14. How many baseball cards can I _____ for a dollar?
    (h e s u r p a c)

15. The top of the building is not _____ in the fog.
    (s i b l i v e)

This Is Super!

Name _____

Super- is a Latin prefix which has several meanings: *over and above, superior to, surpassing, greater than others of its kind,* and *additional.* Use a dictionary to write the definition for each word.

1. superabundant _____

2. superannuated _____

3. supercilious _____

4. superfluous _____

5. supersaturate _____

_____

6. supersonic _____

_____

Answer the questions in complete sentences.

1. Would sending someone ten dozen roses be superfluous or supercilious?

_____

2. Would a jet travel at supersaturated speeds or supersonic speeds?

_____

3. Which would describe a huge crop of peaches: superabundant or supersaturated?

_____

4. If a person is arrogant, is he superfluous or supercilious?

_____

5. Would a retired person be called superannuated or superabundant?

_____

6. Are some foods supersaturated or superannuated with fats?

_____

Sweepstakes Winner!

  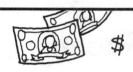

Name _____

Use the Word Box to write the compound word that matches each definition.

1. a lottery – _____

2. a road that winds up an incline – _____

3. United States paper currency – _____

4. terrifying – _____

5. generous – _____

6. a cut of beef – _____

7. sarcastic – _____

8. an obsolete musical instrument – _____

9. something terrible to look at – _____

10. unhappy – _____

11. ordinary – _____

12. electric power shortage – _____

13. a cloth to cover the eyes – _____

14. herding cattle – _____

15. a type of comedy – _____

16. neat and clean – _____

17. a deadlock – _____

18. an exchange – _____

19. heavy eater – _____

Word Box

blindfold	brownout	commonplace	downcast
eyesore	greenback	hair-raising	hornpipe
openhanded	porterhouse	roundup	sharp-tongued
slapstick	stalemate	spic-and-span	tradeoff
sweepstakes	switchback	trencherman	

Help with Homophones

  Name _____

Circle the correct homophones in each sentence.

1. While trying to (undo, undue) the cap, Mom put (undo, undue) pressure on the bottle, causing it to break.

2. Did the city (levee, levy) a tax on boats moored on the (levee, levy)?

3. A runner will sometimes (laps, lapse) into a dreamlike state as he or she runs (laps, lapse) around the track.

4. I was (taught, taut) to keep the rope (taught, taut) on the jib.

5. The (principals, principles) explained the (principals, principles) of education.

6. It was quite a (sight, site) to see the (sight, site) where the space shuttles are launched.

7. Dad (tracked, tract) the elk across a (tracked, tract) of land.

8. It was (shear, sheer) luck that I got to see them (shear, sheer) the sheep yesterday.

9. It was (suite, sweet) of you to let me share your hotel (suite, sweet).

10. It would (seam, seem) that I did not sew this (seam, seem) correctly.

On the lines below, write a sentence for each pair of homophones.

hoarse, horse _____

_____

groan, grown _____

_____

read, reed _____

_____

throne, thrown _____

_____

pause, paws _____

_____

Time for Titles

Name _____

Choose the word from the Word Box that best completes the title for each group of words. Write it on the line.

Word Box

Books	Brave	Cloth	Wetlands
Useless	Hats	Military	Rodents
Ship	Song	Coins	Scientists

Parts of a . . .	Kinds of . . .	Kinds of . . .
_____	_____	_____
gunwale keel rudder	almanac atlas thesaurus	chiffon rayon suede
Kinds of . . .	Words for . . .	Kinds of . . .
_____	_____	_____
peso guinea shilling	gallant courageous dauntless	swamp marsh bog
Kinds of . . .	Officers in the . . .	Parts of a . . .
_____	_____	_____
biologist chemist astronomer	colonel lieutenant general	stanza refrain lyrics
Kinds of . . .	Kinds of . . .	Words for . . .
_____	_____	_____
beret turban fez	muskrat shrew porcupine	fruitless futile unsuccessful

Analyzing Analogies

Name _____

Put an **X** in the circle to show which phrase best completes each analogy.

1. key is to lock as . . .	○ lightbulb is to lamp ○ house is to door
2. cloud is to billowy as . . .	○ rain is to shower ○ cactus is to prickly
3. window is to pane as . . .	○ bookcase is to shelf ○ bumper is to automobile
4. roof is to house as . . .	○ shoe is to sole ○ bow is to boat
5. surgeon is to hospital as . . .	○ priest is to church ○ teacher is to student
6. swim is to pool as . . .	○ read is to library ○ javelin is to discus
7. lawyer is to client as . . .	○ doctor is to hospital ○ banker is to depositor
8. falter is to hesitate as . . .	○ exact is to accurate ○ passage is to passive
9. ornate is to austere as . . .	○ divan is to davenport ○ elegant is to inferior
10. lather is to foam as . . .	○ larceny is to theft ○ prohibit is to permit

You're in Charge!

Name _____

Many words have more than one meaning. Carefully read the meanings for each word. Then write the number in the blank to show how the word is used in each sentence.

charge:
1. to accuse
2. fee
3. responsibility

_____ What is the **charge** for replacing the lost library book?

_____ The baby is my **charge** for the afternoon.

_____ The police will **charge** the woman with robbing the bank.

cast:
1. to fling
2. to deposit
3. to select

_____ Be sure to **cast** your ballot on Election Day.

_____ John will **cast** the fishnet into the ocean.

_____ Martin was **cast** as the king in our class play.

point:
1. the essential idea
2. the exact moment
3. aim

_____ At that **point**, I gave up.

_____ The main **point** of his speech was to give everyone an equal opportunity.

_____ Don't **point** that bow and arrow in this direction.

count:
1. to add up to a total
2. to depend on
3. to include

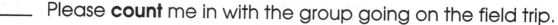

_____ Please **count** me in with the group going on the field trip.

_____ **Count** how many people will be staying for lunch.

_____ I know I can **count** on you when I need help.

The Space Race

Name _____

Build a puzzle using the names of the United States' artificial satellites, space-craft, and manned and unmanned orbiters. The letters already in the puzzle will help you.

Explorer 1
Vanguard
Jupiter
Tiros
Echo
Freedom 7

Friendship 7
Telstar
Mariner
Faith 7
Ranger 7

Gemini
Apollo
Skylab
Pioneer
Viking

STS (Space Transport System – the space shuttles)
ICE (International Cometary Explorer)
Magellan
LDEF (Long Range Exposure Facility)
Galileo
HST (Hubble Space Telescope)
Ulysses
GRO (Gamma Ray Orbiter)

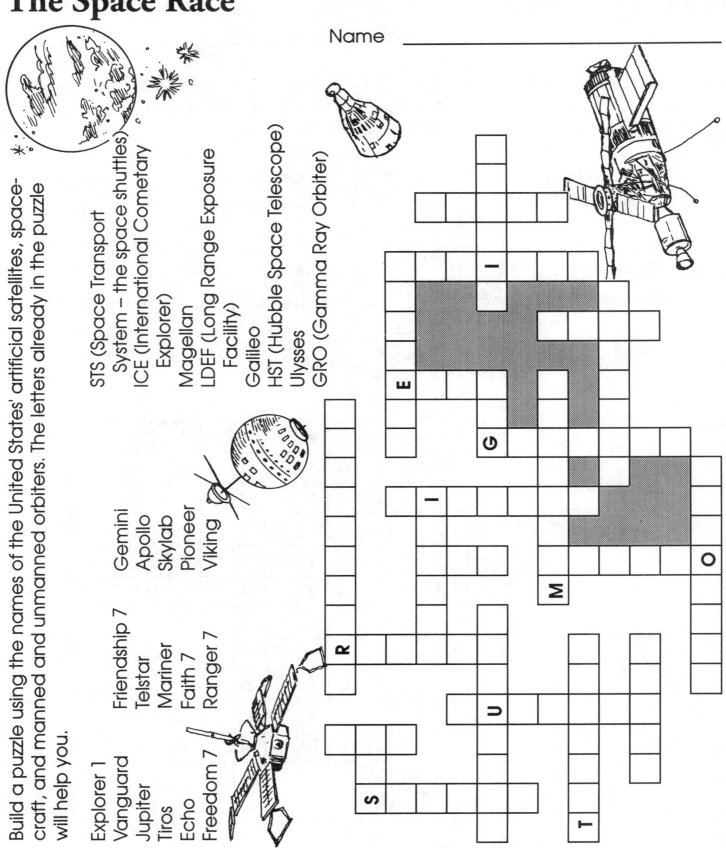

Synonym Search

Name _____

Synonyms are words that mean nearly the same thing. Match the synonyms by writing the correct letter in each blank. Then circle all of the words from both columns in the wordsearch. Words may go → ← ↑ ↓ ↘ ↖ .

_____ 1. encourage

_____ 2. global

_____ 3. maid

_____ 4. rascal

_____ 5. talent

_____ 6. fate

_____ 7. perceive

_____ 8. twitch

_____ 9. precise

_____ 10. grieve

_____ 11. misery

_____ 12. emblem

a. destiny

b. scoundrel

c. exact

d. international

e. mourn

f. agony

g. servant

h. symbol

i. urge

j. ability

k. shudder

l. notice

A	E	I	H	I	K	D	Y	T	I	L	I	B	A	W
J	G	X	N	N	S	H	U	D	D	E	R	L	M	D
O	L	B	A	T	E	C	M	C	E	T	L	P	T	F
N	O	T	I	C	E	G	O	A	P	A	A	R	N	I
R	B	F	L	G	T	R	A	U	I	F	C	E	A	R
U	A	G	O	N	Y	P	N	R	N	D	S	C	V	W
O	L	Q	B	Y	N	T	E	A	U	D	A	I	R	V
M	R	S	M	R	I	T	A	R	T	O	R	S	E	U
E	V	X	Y	E	T	Z	B	L	C	I	C	E	S	T
L	A	C	S	S	S	E	L	G	E	E	O	N	L	O
B	J	P	Q	I	E	Y	M	H	X	N	I	N	E	N
M	A	K	V	M	D	H	C	T	I	W	T	V	A	S
E	R	I	E	G	R	U	Z	G	R	I	E	V	E	L

All Eyes on -ize!

Name _____

The suffix **-ize**, which comes from the Greek suffix **-izen**, has several different meanings: *to cause to be*, *to become like*, *to combine with*, and *to engage in*.

Complete each sentence below with the correct word from the Word Box.

Word Box			
criticize	sterilize	colonize	categorize
idolize	specialize	italicize	realize
victimize	generalize	glamorize	tenderize

1. The dentist will _____ the instruments.

2. The students needed to _____ the list of words.

3. _____ every ship's name.

4. Some people _____ Elvis Presley.

5. A criminal will _____ people.

6. I'll _____ the meat before roasting it.

7. A medical student can _____ in pediatrics.

8. Do you _____ how fortunate you are?

9. This magazine always tries to _____ women.

10. Be specific – don't _____ in your report.

11. People from Europe came to _____ the New World.

12. I wish you wouldn't be so quick to _____ me.

This Is Duck Soup!

Name _____

An **idiom** is a phrase or expression that has a different meaning from its literal definition. For example, something that is "duck soup" is easily accomplished.

Rewrite each sentence using a word or phrase from the Word Box to replace each bold-faced idiom.

Word Box				
deferred	excited	an exaggerator	break	agree
depressed	disbelieve	get angry	clumsy	help

1. I've never seen Jamal so **down in the mouth**.

   _____

2. I **put no stock in** Mr. Smith's claim of being the richest man in town.

   _____

3. My proposal was **put on ice** until the next meeting.

   _____

4. Now, don't **fly off the handle** just because I won't go.

   _____

5. Steven is **all wound up** about Halloween.

   _____

6. Claude and I don't **see eye to eye** on this point.

   _____

7. Please **lend a hand** – this trunk is heavy.

   _____

8. No one believes Carla because she's **full of hot air**.

   _____

9. The teacher said to **take five** before resuming the test.

   _____

10. Don't take Paul shopping – he's **a bull in a china closet**!

    _____

Use the Clues

Name _____

Choose the best word to complete each sentence.

1. I will _____ you if you try that trick again.
    a. array   b. adorn   c. admonish

2. Mr. Perez read us a funny _____ .
    a. anecdote   b. antidote   c. icon

3. Try not to be _____ of Jennifer's new outfit.
    a. inane   b. envious   c. ethical

4. The hurricane brought _____ to the Louisiana coast.
    a. hover   b. hulk   c. havoc

5. Carmen will _____ the play for us.
    a. narrate   b. narrow   c. neglect

6. My computer is already _____ .
    a. obsolete   b. apparent   c. agile

7. Your remark is totally _____ to the topic being discussed.
    a. irresolute   b. irrelevant   c. invitation

8. There was a _____ of artillery fire coming from over the hill.
    a. barracks   b. barnacle   c. barrage

9. Scrooge was an _____ old man.
    a. insulate   b. irascible   c. identical

10. Jane looked very _____ during her illness.
    a. pallid   b. patent   c. pallor

Borrowed from Abroad

Name _____

Many words in the English language have come from other languages. For example, **jar** comes from the Arabic word **jarrah**, which means *earthen container.*

Use a dictionary to find the language from which each of the following words was taken. Write the name of the language and a short meaning for each one.

1. leisure: _____
_____

2. pseudonym: _____
_____

3. semaphore: _____
_____

4. introvert: _____
_____

5. odoriferous: _____
_____

6. harbinger: _____
_____

Answer the following questions in complete sentences.

1. If you wanted to send a message from one ship to another, which would you use: a harbinger or a semaphore?

_____

2. Would a robin be a harbinger or a pseudonym of spring?

_____

3. Would a rose be odoriferous or an introvert?

_____

4. Would a person work or play in his or her leisure time?

_____

Star Light, Star Bright

Name _____

The twenty brightest stars are listed in order of their brightness. Circle their names in the wordsearch. Words may go → ← ↓ ↑ ↖ ↘ ↗↙.

Word Box

Sirius	Procyon	Spica
Canopus	Betelgeuse	Antares
Alpha Centauri	Achernar	Pollux
Arcturus	Beta Centauri	Fomalhaut
Vega	Altair	Deneb
Capella	Alpha Crucis	Beta Crucis
Rigel	Aldebaran	

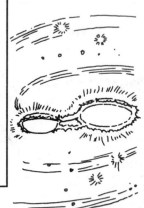

A	R	C	T	U	R	U	S	A	S	R	B	A	L
N	L	I	O	P	O	L	L	U	X	A	E	E	A
A	R	P	R	O	C	Y	O	N	L	N	T	S	L
R	I	E	H	U	R	C	X	R	M	R	A	U	P
A	G	A	D	A	A	O	R	C	A	E	C	E	H
B	E	U	V	P	C	T	S	T	L	H	R	G	A
E	L	V	E	G	A	E	N	U	F	C	U	L	C
D	T	L	O	L	D	E	N	E	B	A	C	E	R
L	L	X	T	A	V	I	R	T	C	T	I	T	U
A	R	A	S	N	X	O	N	I	A	A	S	E	C
L	I	E	C	A	N	O	P	U	S	U	T	B	I
R	S	U	I	R	I	S	A	N	T	A	R	E	S
S	T	A	T	U	A	H	L	A	M	O	F	I	B

Produce the Produce

Name _____

PRONUNCIATIONS

insult (in sult´)
    (in´ sult)

progress (präg´ res)
    (prə gres´)

wound (wo͞ond)
    (wound)

produce (prə do͞os´)
    (prō´ do͞os)

reject (ri jekt´)
    (rē jekt)

permit (pər mit´)
    (pur´ mit)

resume (ri zo͞om´)
    (rez´ oo mā´)

separate (sep´ ə rāt´)
    (sep´ rit)

Write the pronunciation for each word in bold-faced type.

1. His **insult** (_____) was meant to **insult** (_____) me.

2. We can't make any **progress** (_____) unless you're willing to
   progress (_____) to the next step.

3. The nurse **wound** (_____) the bandage around the **wound**
   (_____).

4. Did the farmer **produce** (_____) all of that **produce**
   (_____) on his farm?

5. He might **reject** (_____) any ideas of what to do with the
   reject (_____).

6. The police will **permit** (_____) you to park here if you have a
   valid **permit** (_____).

7. You can **resume** (_____) writing your **resume** (_____).

8. Please **separate** (_____) the laundry into two **separate**
   (_____) loads.

Weird Words

Name _____

Use a dictionary to answer the questions using complete sentences.

1. Would a king be seen in his jalopy or his regalia?

   _____

2. Is the study of aging called gerontology or astronomy?

   _____

3. Would a building be likely to have a regalia or a canopy?

   _____

4. Which is something to eat: a canopy or consommé?

   _____

5. Is a bean an example of a legume or a legacy?

   _____

6. Which might you receive from your grandmother: a legacy or a matinee?

   _____

7. Would a young person or an old person be more likely to try to rejuvenate himself or herself?

   _____

8. Which would a teenager drive: a legume or a jalopy?

   _____

9. If you go to a play in the afternoon, are you attending the matinee or the consommé performance?

   _____

10. What would you study in an astronomy class?

    _____

Crossword Careers

Name _____

Build a puzzle with the career names in the Word Box. **Hint:** Build off **electrician**.

Word Box

engineer	judge	nurse	pilot	artist	mechanic
banker	lawyer	singer	chemist	dentist	architect
plumber	teacher	clerk	author	painter	astronaut

You're Too Smart for Me!

Name _____

Many words have more than one meaning. Carefully read the meanings for each word. Then write the number in the blank to show how the word is used in each sentence.

smart: 1. clever, intelligent
2. sting
3. stylish

____ Mother wore a **smart** new outfit on the trip.

____ It will **smart** if you put iodine on the cut.

____ You're too **smart** for me!

block: 1. section of buildings
2. obstruct
3. a solid piece of stone

____ Please don't **block** the driveway with your bicycle.

____ The pharmacy is in the next **block**.

____ The artist will chisel the statue from the **block** of marble.

sound: 1. activate
2. to say distinctly
3. earshot

____ Are you within the **sound** of my voice?

____ I'll try to **sound** out the new vocabulary word.

____ **Sound** the alarm! The building is on fire.

brush: 1. to apply
2. scrub growth
3. knock

____ **Brush** the paint in only one direction.

____ Let's clear the vacant lot of all this **brush**.

____ I hope I don't **brush** the crystal goblet off the table.

It's All Greek to Me!

Name _____

Use a dictionary to find from what language each word in the Word Box was taken. Write each word in the correct category. Then choose one word from each category and use it in a sentence.

Word Box

ballet	autograph	ballot	carom	clamp	cookie
coral	coroner	detach	feather	furlough	gambit
glitzy	horror	osmosis	parasol	prodigal	revenge
roan	schnauzer	sneeze	soprano	tribute	psyche

Greek
_____
_____
_____
_____

Italian
_____
_____
_____
_____

French
_____
_____
_____
_____

English
_____
_____
_____
_____

Spanish
_____
_____

German
_____
_____

Latin
_____
_____
_____

Dutch
_____
_____
_____

1. _____
2. _____
3. _____
4. _____
5. _____
6. _____
7. _____
8. _____

This Is New to Me!

Name _____

Rewrite each sentence below, replacing the word **new** with one of the synonyms given. Since the synonyms have slight differences in meanings, be careful to choose the correct one.

new: additional, fresh, original, unfamiliar, unprecedented

1. The lawyer said she would need **new** evidence if she hoped to win the case.

   _____

   _____

2. I hope I don't get lost — this road is **new** to me.

   _____

3. Daniel's experiment must be **new** to win first place in the Science Fair.

   _____

   _____

4. In a **new** move, the President named the first woman to his cabinet.

   _____

   _____

5. How do you like the **new** potatoes that I just dug out of the garden?

   _____

   _____

Get in Shape!

Name _____

Use the code to write a synonym for each word. Follow the example.

t	p	a
s	e	l

Example: say – ┘⊓┌┌   <u>tell</u>

1. flavor – ┘└┐┘⊓   _____
2. decline – ┌└⊔┐⊓   _____
3. overtake – ⊔└┐┐   _____
4. pilfer – ┐┘⊓└┌   _____
5. satisfy – └⊔⊔⊓└┐⊓   _____
6. fewest – ┌⊓└┐┘   _____
7. strike – ┐┌└⊔   _____
8. spaghetti – ⊔└┐┘└   _____
9. tardy – ┌└┘⊓   _____
10. fold – ⊔┌⊓└┘   _____
11. favorite – ⊔⊓┘   _____
12. hide – ⊔⊓┌┘   _____
13. skin – ⊔⊓⊓┌   _____
14. final – ┌└┐┘   _____
15. rap – ┘└⊔   _____
16. ring – ⊔⊓└┌   _____
17. former – ⊔└┐┘   _____
18. relieve – ⊓└┐⊓   _____
19. ingest – ⊓└┘   _____
20. chair – ┐⊓└┘   _____
21. spirit – ⊔⊓⊔   _____
22. jump – ┌⊓└⊔   _____

24   IF5025 Vocabulary Enrichment

What Will Transpire Here?

Name _____

Trans- if a Latin prefix that means *over*, *beyond*, or *across*. Write the correct word from the Word Box in each sentence.

Word Box			
transcribe	transfer	transit	transparent
transcend	transform	translucent	transpire
transact	transient	transmit	transport

1. Mrs. Johnson put _____ tape on the torn page.

2. When we move, I will have to _____ to another school.

3. Mr. Kwan came to the United States to _____ business.

4. Do you think it's possible to _____ this piece of marble into a statue of Lincoln?

5. Mr. Davis will need to _____ his shorthand notes for us.

6. Perhaps this performance will _____ all others this year.

7. The sheer curtains at the window are _____ .

8. Can you _____ the message over a short-wave radio?

9. I think Shamara is in _____ somewhere between New York and Philadelphia.

10. We will need to _____ the heaviest boxes in a truck.

11. What do you think will _____ during the president's meeting?

12. The _____ will probably only stay a day before moving on to the next town.

You're Wise to Categorize

ginko mahongany sequoia

Name _____

Choose the word or phrase from the Word Box that best completes the heading for each group of words.

Word Box

Electric Motor	Birds	Atom	Bones
Card Games	Clever	Dogs	Fight
Stubborn	Shorten	Trees	Trip

Other words for . . .	Kinds of . . .	Parts of an . . .
_____	_____	_____
safari	scapula	neutron
expedition	humerus	nucleus
journey	clavicle	electron

Parts of an . . .	Other words for . . .	Kinds of . . .
_____	_____	_____
armature	restrict	gingko
shaft	reduce	mahogany
commutator	condense	sequoia

Other words for . . .	Kinds of . . .	Kinds of . . .
_____	_____	_____
bright	bridge	terrier
sharp	rummy	spaniel
keen	pinochle	Dalmation

Other words for . . .	Other words for . . .	Kinds of . . .
_____	_____	_____
struggle	inflexible	puffin
conflict	cantankerous	snipe
riot	obstinate	starling

You're a Pro!

Name _____

The Latin prefix **pro-** has several meanings: *moving forward, substituting for,* and *supporting*. Match each word with its meaning by writing the correct letter in the blank.

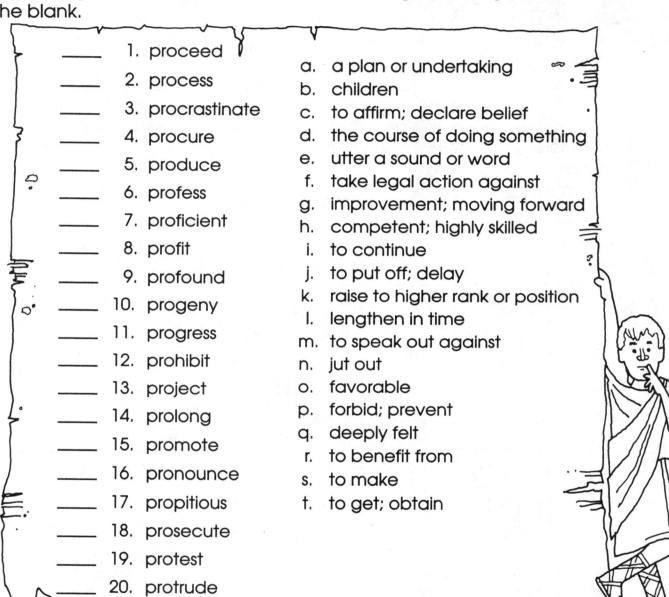

_____ 1. proceed
_____ 2. process
_____ 3. procrastinate
_____ 4. procure
_____ 5. produce
_____ 6. profess
_____ 7. proficient
_____ 8. profit
_____ 9. profound
_____ 10. progeny
_____ 11. progress
_____ 12. prohibit
_____ 13. project
_____ 14. prolong
_____ 15. promote
_____ 16. pronounce
_____ 17. propitious
_____ 18. prosecute
_____ 19. protest
_____ 20. protrude

a. a plan or undertaking
b. children
c. to affirm; declare belief
d. the course of doing something
e. utter a sound or word
f. take legal action against
g. improvement; moving forward
h. competent; highly skilled
i. to continue
j. to put off; delay
k. raise to higher rank or position
l. lengthen in time
m. to speak out against
n. jut out
o. favorable
p. forbid; prevent
q. deeply felt
r. to benefit from
s. to make
t. to get; obtain

Write a sentence for each word below.

1. promise _____

2. protect _____

3. pronoun _____

4. propel _____

Make No Bones About It

Name _____

Your body has over 200 bones. In the wordsearch, circle the names of the bones listed below. Words may go → ← ↑ ↓ ↖ ↘.

maxilla	ribs	pubis	patella
mandible	humerus	carpals	fibula
clavicle	vertebrae	metacarpal	tibia
scapula	ulna	phalanges	tarsals
sternum	radius	femur	metatarsals

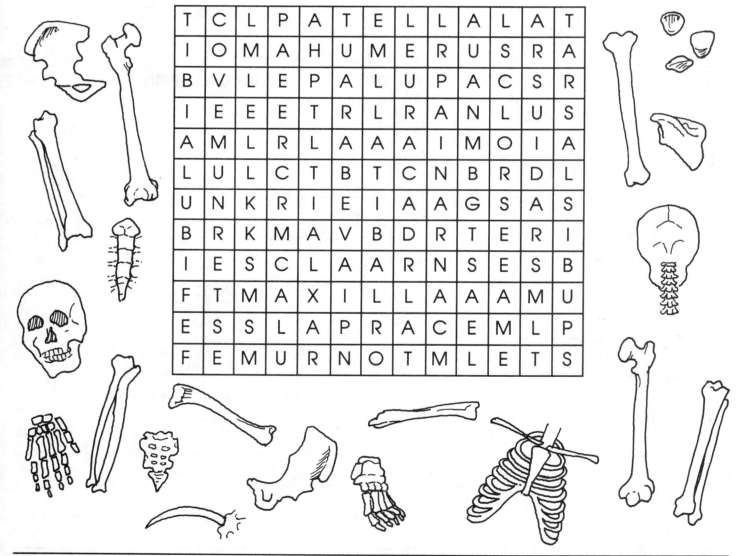

T	C	L	P	A	T	E	L	L	A	L	A	T
I	O	M	A	H	U	M	E	R	U	S	R	A
B	V	L	E	P	A	L	U	P	A	C	S	R
I	E	E	E	T	R	L	R	A	N	L	U	S
A	M	L	R	L	A	A	A	I	M	O	I	A
L	U	L	C	T	B	T	C	N	B	R	D	L
U	N	K	R	I	E	I	A	A	G	S	A	S
B	R	K	M	A	V	B	D	R	T	E	R	I
I	E	S	C	L	A	A	R	N	S	E	S	B
F	T	M	A	X	I	L	L	A	A	A	M	U
E	S	S	L	A	P	R	A	C	E	M	L	P
F	E	M	U	R	N	O	T	M	L	E	T	S

súmapplesorry

Out of Sight!

idioms

Name _____

An **idiom** is a phrase or expression that has a different meaning from its literal definition. For example, "Out of Sight!" means *outrageous*.

Rewrite each sentence using a word or phrase from the Word Box to replace each bold-faced idiom.

Word Box				
clean	clumsy	declined	defend	dictate
discredited	frightened me	inexperienced	unconscious	thin

1. The new teacher was **wet behind the ears**.

   _____

2. That science fiction movie **made my blood run cold**.

   _____

3. Dad **turned thumbs down on** my offer to help him.

   _____

4. Don't let Cory always **run the show**.

   _____

5. Grandmother is **all skin and bones**.

   _____

6. The boxer was **out like a light**.

   _____

7. Margo appears to be **all thumbs**.

   _____

8. I'll **speak up for** my right to represent the class.

   _____

9. We have to **straighten up the house** today.

   _____

10. My idea for having a soda machine in class got **shot full of holes**.

   _____

Similar in Some Way

Name _____

Put an **X** in the circle beside the phrase that correctly completes each analogy.

1. saunter is to stroll as . . .	○ discreet is to tactful ○ sensible is to foolish
2. ferocious is to gentle as . . .	○ descend is to lower ○ profit is to loss
3. plague is to epidemic as . . .	○ cliff is to precipice ○ loose is to tight
4. harbor is to haven as . . .	○ deserve is to merit ○ delete is to add
5. connect is to detach as . . .	○ unique is to ordinary ○ defy is to dare
6. flaunt is to brandish as . . .	○ nourish is to sustain ○ improper is to decent
7. apparel is to attire as . . .	○ honest is to deceit ○ dribble is to trickle
8. specific is to general as . . .	○ familiar is to foreign ○ collapse is to downfall
9. exceed is to surpass as . . .	○ desert is to abandon ○ straight is to crooked
10. create is to destroy as . . .	○ collect is to gather ○ employ is to dismiss
11. peer is to gaze as . . .	○ eerie is to weird ○ calm is to nervous

Don't Get in a Stew Over This

DICTIONARY   Name _____

From which culture do you think each of these food words came? Write your guess in Column A. Then use the dictionary to check your guess. Write that answer in Column B.

Word Box				
Native American	Aztec	Arabic	Chinese	Old English
French	German	Italian	Mexican	Persian
Spanish	West African			

		A		B
1. banana		_____		_____
2. canapé		_____		_____
3. candy		_____		_____
4. chicken		_____		_____
5. chocolate		_____		_____
6. chow mein		_____		_____
7. coffee		_____		_____
8. éclair		_____		_____
9. fricassee		_____		_____
10. hamburger		_____		_____
11. pasta		_____		_____
12. pecan		_____		_____
13. pizza		_____		_____
14. pone		_____		_____
15. shish kebab		_____		_____
16. spaghetti		_____		_____
17. succotash		_____		_____
18. taco		_____		_____
19. tortilla		_____		_____
20. won ton		_____		_____

Simply Synonyms

Name _____

In each set, only two of the words are synonyms. Cross out the one that is not. Then write a sentence using one of the synonyms correctly.

1.   extend   expand   exchange

_____

2.   aggressive   admonish   assertive

_____

3.   obnoxious   obvious   apparent

_____

4.   corrupt   condemn   dishonest

_____

5.   fluid   liquid   stable

_____

6.   nourish   loathe   despise

_____

7.   modest   monotonous   boring

_____

8.   cool   nonchalant   tense

_____

9.   pliable   flexible   irritable

_____

10.   trivial   wrangle   quarrel

_____

11.   lethargic   energetic   vigorous

_____

12.   drivel   drool   revival

_____

This Is So Fine

Name _____

Rewrite each sentence below, replacing the word **fine** with one of the synonyms given. Since the synonyms have slight differences in meaning, be careful to choose the correct one.

> **fine:**   clear, delicate, elegant, excellent, small, sharp, subtle

1. That was a **fine** dinner we enjoyed at your home.

   _____

   _____

2. I wash this blouse by hand because of its **fine** lace collar.

   _____

   _____

3. The sand in an hourglass must be very **fine** to trickle as it does.

   _____

   _____

4. We need **fine** weather for sailing.

   _____

   _____

5. Dad used a whetstone to put a **fine** edge on the knife.

   _____

   _____

6. Sometimes there is a **fine** line between innocence and guilt.

   _____

   _____

7. The queen wore a **fine** gown encrusted with jewels.

   _____

   _____

Are You in Your Element?

 Name _____

There are over one hundred known chemical elements. Use an encyclopedia to write each element from the Word Box in the correct category. Then circle the elements in the wordsearch. Words may go → ← ↑ ↓ ↘ ↖ .

Word Box

arsenic	barium	boron	calcium	carbon	chlorine
fluorine	iodine	lithium	magnesium	nitrogen	oxygen
phosphorus	potassium	radium	silicon	sodium	sulfur

Nonmetals

_____   _____

_____   _____

_____   _____

_____   _____

_____

Metals

_____   _____

_____   _____

_____   _____

_____   _____

Oxygen 8 — O — 16.000

Fluorine 9 — F — 19.00

M	M	P	L	I	T	H	I	U	M	F	M	F
N	A	U	H	M	U	I	D	O	S	L	U	L
C	E	G	I	O	X	Y	G	E	N	U	N	U
H	N	G	N	S	S	T	A	L	O	O	N	O
L	I	K	O	E	S	P	C	O	R	R	O	R
O	D	C	S	R	S	A	H	R	O	I	C	I
R	O	A	E	G	T	I	T	O	B	N	I	D
I	I	L	T	Y	N	I	U	O	R	E	L	E
N	O	C	A	R	B	O	N	M	P	U	I	C
E	R	I	R	B	R	R	U	F	L	U	S	L
I	M	U	I	R	A	B	S	E	L	P	P	A
T	S	M	U	I	D	A	R	S	E	N	I	C

Quite a (Feat, Feet)!

Name _____

Circle the correct homophones in each sentence.

1. It was quite a (feat, feet) to jump 18 (feat, feet) in the long jump.

2. The mayor went before the (council, counsel) to (council, counsel) them about the new laws.

3. I will (ascent, assent) to try the (ascent, assent) of Mount Everest.

4. How can you be so (callous, callus) about my painful (callous, callus)?

5. You are sure to receive a (complement, compliment) if you (complement, compliment) that piece of pie with a scoop of ice cream.

6. There is a (roomer, rumor) that the new (roomer, rumor) at the boarding-house is from China.

7. The liquid in that (vial, vile) tastes (vial, vile) to me

8. Can you imagine what would (cause, caws) the crow's loud (cause, caws)?

9. On what do you (base, bass) your opinion that the (base, bass) is the best instrument?

10. The knight admitted his (gilt, guilt) of taking the sword covered with (gilt, guilt).

On the lines below, write a sentence for each pair of homophones.

not, knot _____

_____

main, mane _____

_____

mail, male _____

_____

weak, week _____

_____

sighs, size _____

_____

Title Time

Name _____

Choose the word or phrase from the Word Box that best completes the heading for each group of words.

Word Box			
Cell	Dances	Eye	Fierce
Flower	Gems	Red	Shapes
Speech	Teeth	Weird	Sporting Events

Places for . . .	Names of . . .	Parts of a . . .
_____	_____	_____
arena natatorium coliseum	bicuspid molar incisor	pistil stamen sepal

Parts of a . . .	Kinds of . . .	Other words for . . .
_____	_____	_____
nucleus cytoplasm chloroplasts	trapezoid octagon parallelogram	uncanny peculiar strange

Kinds of . . .	Parts of . . .	Shades of . . .
_____	_____	_____
opal topaz peridot	conjunction participle preposition	vermilion crimson scarlet

Words for . . .	Kinds of . . .	Parts of the . . .
_____	_____	_____
feral bestial vicious	jig minuet bolero	cornea lens retina

The Subject Is Homograph

Name _____

PRONUNCIATIONS		
compact (kəm pakt´) (käm´ pakt)	**conflict** (kən flikt´) (kän´ flikt)	**convert** (kən vərt´) (kän´ vərt)
present (prez´ nt) (pri zent´)	**rebel** (reb´ l) (ri bel´)	**subject** (sub´ jikt) (səb jekt´)
suspect (sə spekt´) (sus´ pekt)	**transport** (trans pôrt´) (trans´ pôrt)	**use** (yo͞os) (yo͞oz)

Write the correct pronunciation for each word in bold-faced type.

1. Surely you are not going to **subject** (_____) me to any more of that **subject** (_____).

2. The factory will **transport** (_____) the new cars on a **transport** (_____) truck.

3. Would you please **present** (_____) the **present** (_____) to George now?

4. It is the nature of a **rebel** (_____) to **rebel** (_____) against authority.

5. I **suspect** (_____) the **suspect** (_____) has been in trouble before.

6. Could you **use** (_____) this rope for another **use** (_____)?

7. The **convert** (_____) may try to **convert** (_____) others to his cause.

8. How do they **compact** (_____) face powder to make it stay in a **compact** (_____)?

9. Our ideas **conflict** (_____) on how to end the **conflict** (_____).

Analyze These Analogies

Name _____

Put an **X** in the circle by the phrase to correctly complete each analogy.

1. ax is to chop as . . .	◯ measure is to ruler ◯ scissors is to cut
2. peach is to tree as . . .	◯ broccoli is to asparagus ◯ cucumber is to vine
3. marathon is to runner as . . .	◯ regatta is to sailor ◯ gymnast is to tumbling
4. racket is to tennis as . . .	◯ club is to golf ◯ jockey is to horse
5. scientist is to laboratory as . . .	◯ bathyscaph is to diver ◯ astronaut is to spacecraft
6. odious is to disgusting as . . .	◯ morose is to gloomy ◯ moron is to intellectual
7. throw is to pitch as . . .	◯ kick is to punt ◯ basket is to basketball
8. shaky is to tremulous as . . .	◯ vertical is to horizontal ◯ isolate is to sequester
9. scalpel is to surgeon as . . .	◯ bookmobile is to library ◯ wrench is to plumber
10. spaghetti is to pasta as . . .	◯ sausage is to bacon ◯ kumquat is to fruit
11. koala is to marsupial as . . .	◯ porcupine is to rodent ◯ emu is to pelican

Watch Out!

Name _____

Match the correct definition to each word beginning with **out-**.

_____ 1. outage
_____ 2. outback
_____ 3. outbid
_____ 4. outboard
_____ 5. outbreak
_____ 6. outburst
_____ 7. outcast
_____ 8. outclass
_____ 9. outcome
_____ 10. outcry
_____ 11. outdoors
_____ 12. outfield
_____ 13. outfit
_____ 14. outlaw
_____ 15. outlay
_____ 16. outlet
_____ 17. outlive
_____ 18. outlook
_____ 19. outmoded
_____ 20. outpost
_____ 21. output
_____ 22. outrage
_____ 23. outreach
_____ 24. outright

a. a rejected person
b. clothes worn together
c. market for specific goods
d. amount produced
e. accidental loss of electric power
f. result
g. no longer fashionable
h. to extend
i. to offer more
j. sudden release of emotion
k. playing area beyond infield
l. criminal
m. viewpoint
n. extremely violent act
o. straightforward
p. Australia's wild inland region
q. outside the boat
r. strong protest
s. money spent
t. base away from home
u. sudden occurence
v. to surpass
w. endure longer than
x. in the open

What's in a Name?

Name _____

Use the Word Box and the clues to work the crossword puzzle and find out the origin of some words.

Word Box
coat
port
tomb
roof
coach
abode
graham
patriot
hackney
paisley
maudlin
marathon
sandwich
governor
saxophone
pompadour

Across

2. an instrument named after a 19th century Belgian inventor, Sax
3. the word mayonnaise came from the name of a _____ on a Spanish island
5. the word mausoleum came from the _____ of King Mausolus
7. a kind of cracker named after a 19th century American dietician
9. patterned cloth named after a place in Scotland
11. the word pandemonium is from the name of the demon's _____ in Milton's book *Paradise Lost*
13. a chesterfield is a _____ named after the Earl of Chesterfield
14. _____ is a kind of horse that came from a town in England

Down

1. a hairdo named after a French woman
3. the word chauvinism came from Chauvin, a fanatic French _____
4. a food name that came from the name of an English earl
6. a kind of race named for a place in ancient Greece
7. the word gerrymander came in part from Elbridge Gerry, a _____ of Massachusetts
8. the word _____ came from Mary Magdalene, a woman in the Bible, often represented weeping
10. a kind of _____ was named after Mansard, a 17th century French architect
12. a carriage named after the Hungarian village of Kócs

Crackerjack Wordsearch

Name _____

Circle all the words containing the **ck** digraph in the wordsearch.

Word Box

sack	track	snack	racket	bracket
back	slick	brick	hockey	backward
lock	slack	stack	cackle	crackpot
lick	smack	socks	beckon	sprocket
luck	stock	crack	jockey	necklace
pack	speck	tacks	pocket	bareback
peck	wreck	stick	jacket	checkers
tuck	pluck	black	attack	cockroach
lack	clock	rocket	cracker	woodpecker
hack	rocky	locket	crackle	crackerjack
rack				

C	R	A	C	K	E	R	J	A	C	K	C	I	L	S	R
R	E	K	C	E	P	D	O	O	W	L	S	A	C	K	O
A	O	B	C	R	A	C	K	P	O	T	U	C	K	E	C
C	M	C	A	S	T	E	K	C	O	R	P	S	L	P	K
K	S	K	K	R	R	O	K	C	I	L	P	K	A	K	Y
E	M	C	X	E	E	E	K	C	A	L	C	C	C	E	T
R	A	E	L	S	T	B	K	R	U	A	K	I	K	Y	S
R	C	P	K	S	O	N	A	C	R	O	R	C	E	T	T
I	K	C	K	N	N	O	K	C	E	B	O	K	N	E	E
Z	O	C	M	A	T	T	A	C	K	H	C	E	K	K	K
S	A	T	H	C	A	O	R	K	C	O	C	C	B	C	C
T	R	A	C	K	C	A	H	A	J	K	A	L	A	A	O
I	M	W	R	E	C	K	C	U	L	R	A	T	C	R	P
C	I	D	R	A	W	K	C	A	B	C	T	I	K	R	A
K	C	A	L	S	L	O	C	K	K	A	K	C	O	L	C
J	A	C	K	E	T	E	K	C	E	P	S	T	A	C	K

Explore Context Clues

Name _____

Unscramble the letters in parentheses to spell a word that makes sense in each sentence. The first letter of the word is underlined.

1. Come, let's _____ this cave.
   (r <u>e</u> x l o p e)

2. The dying man showed a lot of _____ .
   (r o g u a <u>c</u> e)

3. How can I _____ you that I am right?
   (o n n i v e <u>c</u> c)

4. I feel so _____ that I'm going to take a nap.
   (s y o <u>d</u> w r)

5. The soldier was held _____ in the jungle for a year.
   (t a p v i <u>c</u> e)

6. I heard reindeer _____ prancing on the roof.
   (s o v e <u>h</u> o)

7. I plan to _____ from college next year.
   (e d r u a <u>g</u> a t)

8. You need a _____ before class pictures are taken.
   (a r c <u>h</u> u i t)

9. Was Bill _____ when his brother won first place?
   (s e u l o a <u>j</u>)

10. Two _____ were missing from the silverware drawer.
    (v i s <u>k</u> e n)

11. I yelled so much at the pep rally that I got _____ .
    (s o r e a <u>h</u>)

12. The _____ isn't large enough for our new van.
    (a r a g <u>g</u> e)

13. I can only hope that my grades will _____ .
    (r o p v <u>i</u> e m)

14. Dad backed the car into the fire _____ .
    (t a n d r y <u>h</u>)

15. Is it in _____ to wear stripes with plaids?
    (n o s i <u>f</u> a h)

Antonym Action

Name _____

Antonyms are words with opposite meanings. Match the antonyms by writing the correct letter in each blank.

a. attractive	____ 1. accumulate
b. vain	____ 2. lethargic
c. unbearable	____ 3. repulsive
d. dissipate	____ 4. spurious
e. remiss	____ 5. modest
f. authentic	____ 6. scrupulous
g. vigorous	____ 7. endurable
h. flattering	____ 8. unbecoming
i. insufficient	____ 9. superficial
j. goodwill	____ 10. adequate
k. biased	____ 11. beneficial
l. exhaustive	____ 12. animosity
m. uninteresting	____ 13. objective
n. harmful	____ 14. engrossing

Write a sentence for each of the following words.

lethargic _____

_____

animosity _____

_____

superficial _____

_____

beneficial _____

_____

Answer Key
Vocabulary Enrichment
Grade 5

Name _____

Mountains are many different shapes and sizes. Build a puzzle with the names of some of the most famous mountains on earth. Hint: Build off Aconcagua first.

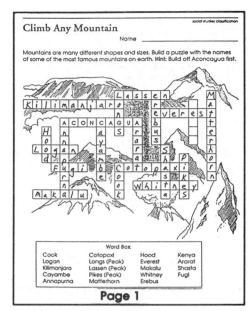

Word Box

Cook	Cotopaxi	Hood	Kenya
Logan	Longs (Peak)	Everest	Ararat
Kilimanjaro	Lassen (Peak)	Makalu	Shasta
Cayambe	Pikes (Peak)	Whitney	Fuji
Annapurna	Matterhorn	Erebus	

Page 1

Palindromes – Wow!

Name _____

A palindrome is a word that reads the same backward and forward. Use the words in the Word Box to complete the sentences.

Word Box

bob	deed	civic	level
nun	peep	radar	refer
ewe	kayak	redder	solos

1. It is your _civic_ duty to vote in the election.
2. Please _refer_ to your dictionary for the correct spelling of that word.
3. The longer I stay in the sun, the _redder_ I get.
4. Don't you dare let me hear a _peep_ out of you.
5. Do you like to _bob_ for apples on Halloween?
6. The _kayak_, an Eskimo canoe, is made of skins on a wooden frame.
7. The _ewe_ and the ram have woolly coats.
8. Gino was awarded a medal for his brave _deed_.
9. My sister is a _nun_ and teaches elementary school.
10. Do you see the plane on the _radar_ screen?
11. Have you sung many _solos_ before?
12. The land was _level_ for as far as one could see.

Think of three palindromes of your own and write a sentence for each one.

_____
_____
_____

Page 2

Code Names

Name _____

Use the code to write a synonym for each word.

a	c	e	i	l	m	n	o	p	q	r	s	t	u	v	x	y	z
1	2	3	4	5	6	7	8	9	10	11	12	13	14	15	16	17	17

1. surprise – _amaze_
2. anticipate – _expect_
3. concern – _anxiety_
4. forgive – _excuse_
5. screwy – _insane_
6. tempt – _entice_
7. expect – _assume_
8. thorough – _intensive_
9. eat – _consume_
10. cross – _intersect_
11. slight – _petty_
12. inactive – _passive_
13. match – _equate_
14. sorry – _penitent_
15. rude – _sassy_
16. fragrance – _scent_
17. delicate – _sensitive_
18. truthful – _veracious_
19. impatient – _testy_
20. follow – _ensue_

Using the same code given at the top of the page, write five more words and the code numbers for their synonyms. Trade papers with a classmate and decipher each other's code words.

Example: penny – _cent_

1. _____   4. _____
2. _____   5. _____
3. _____

Page 3

Scrambled Words

Name _____

Unscramble the letters in parentheses to spell a word that makes sense in each sentence. Write the word in the blank.

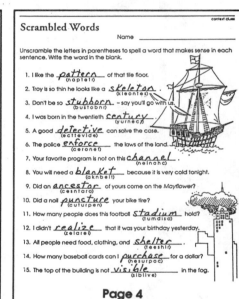

1. I like the _pattern_ of that tile floor. (naptet)
2. Troy is so thin he looks like a _skeleton_. (kleontes)
3. Don't be so _stubborn_ – say you'll go with us. (bustobn)
4. I was born in the twentieth _century_. (yurnec)
5. A good _detective_ can solve the case. (ecttevlde)
6. The police _enforce_ the laws of the land. (cerone)
7. Your favorite program is not on this _channel_. (neinahc)
8. You will need a _blanket_ because it is very cold tonight. (aknbelt)
9. Did an _ancestor_ of yours come on the *Mayflower*? (csentara)
10. Did a nail _puncture_ your bike tire? (cuturpen)
11. How many people does this football _stadium_ hold? (tumdisa)
12. I didn't _realize_ that it was your birthday yesterday. (zelared)
13. All people need food, clothing, and _shelter_. (teeshl)
14. How many baseball cards can I _purchase_ for a dollar? (hesurpac)
15. The top of the building is not _visible_ in the fog. (isblive)

Page 4

This Is Super!

Name _____

Super- is a Latin prefix which has several meanings: *over and above, superior to, surpassing, greater than others of its kind,* and *additional.* Use a dictionary to write the definition for each word.

1. superabundant _more than enough_
2. superannuated _too old to work_
3. supercilious _disdainful; contemptuous; haughty_
4. superfluous _unnecessary; excessive_
5. supersaturate _to make more concentrated than in normal saturation_
6. supersonic _moving at or faster than the speed of sound_

Answer the questions in complete sentences.

1. Would sending someone ten dozen roses be superfluous or supercilious?
It would be superfluous.
2. Would a jet travel at supersaturated speeds or supersonic speeds?
It would travel at supersonic speeds.
3. Which would describe a huge crop of peaches: superabundant or supersaturated?
The crop would be superabundant.
4. If a person is arrogant, is he superfluous or supercilious?
The person is supercilious.
5. Would a retired person be called superannuated or superabundant?
The person would be superannuated.
6. Are some foods supersaturated or superannuated with fats?
They are supersaturated.

Page 5

Sweepstakes Winner!

Name _____

Use the Word Box to write the compound word that matches each definition.

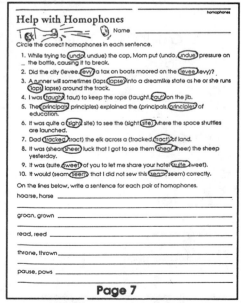

1. a lottery – _sweepstakes_
2. a road that winds up an incline – _switchback_
3. United States paper currency – _greenback_
4. terrifying – _hair-raising_
5. generous – _openhanded_
6. a cut of beef – _porterhouse_
7. sarcastic – _sharp-tongued_
8. an obsolete musical instrument – _hornpipe_
9. something terrible to look at – _eyesore_
10. unhappy – _downcast_
11. ordinary – _commonplace_
12. electric power shortage – _brownout_
13. a cloth to cover the eyes – _blindfold_
14. herding cattle – _roundup_
15. a type of comedy – _slapstick_
16. neat and clean – _spic-and-span_
17. d deadlock – _stalemate_
18. to exchange – _tradeoff_
19. heavy eater – _trencherman_

Word Box

blindfold	brownout	commonplace	downcast
eyesore	greenback	hair-raising	hornpipe
openhanded	porterhouse	roundup	sharp-tongued
slapstick	stalemate	spic-and-span	tradeoff
sweepstakes	switchback	trencherman	

Page 6

Help with Homophones

Name _____

Circle the correct homophones in each sentence.

1. While trying to (undo, undue) the cap, Mom put (undo, **undue**) pressure on the bottle, causing it to break.
2. Did the city (levee, **levy**) a tax on boats moored on the (**levee**, levy)?
3. A runner will sometimes (laps, **lapse**) into a dreamlike state as he or she runs (**laps**, lapse) around the track.
4. I was (**taught**, taut) to keep the rope (taught, **taut**) on the jib.
5. The (**principals**, principles) explained the (principals, **principles**) of education.
6. It is quite a (**sight**, site) to see the (sight, **site**) where the space shuttles are launched.
7. Dad (**tracked**, tract) the elk across a (tracked, **tract**) of land.
8. It was (shear, **sheer**) luck that I got to see them (**shear**, sheer) the sheep yesterday.
9. It was (suite, **sweet**) of you to let me share your hotel (**suite**, sweet).
10. It would (seam, **seem**) that I did not sew this (**seam**, seem) correctly.

On the lines below, write a sentence for each pair of homophones.

hoarse, horse _____

groan, grown _____

read, reed _____

throne, thrown _____

pause, paws _____

Page 7

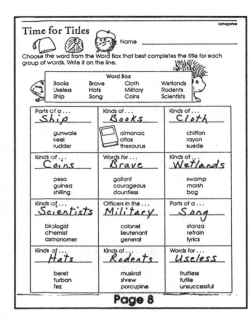

Time for Titles

Choose the word from the Word Box that best completes the title for each group of words. Write it on the line.

Word Box

Books	Brave	Cloth	Wetlands
Useless	Hats	Military	Rodents
Ship	Song	Coins	Scientists

Parts of a... **Ship**
gunwale
keel
rudder

Kinds of... **Books**
almanac
atlas
thesaurus

Kinds of... **Cloth**
chiffon
rayon
suede

Kinds of... **Coins**
peso
guinea
shilling

Words for... **Brave**
gallant
courageous
dauntless

Kinds of... **Wetlands**
swamp
marsh
bog

Kinds of... **Scientists**
biologist
chemist
astronomer

Officers in the... **Military**
colonel
lieutenant
general

Parts of a... **Song**
stanza
refrain
lyrics

Kinds of... **Hats**
beret
turban
fez

Kinds of... **Rodents**
muskrat
shrew
porcupine

Words for... **Useless**
fruitless
futile
unsuccessful

Page 8

Analyzing Analogies

Put an X in the circle to show which phrase best completes each analogy.

1. key is to lock as... ⊗ lightbulb is to lamp / ○ house is to door
2. cloud is to billowy as... ○ rain is to shower / ⊗ cactus is to prickly
3. window is to pane as... ⊗ bookcase is to shelf / ○ bumper is to automobile
4. roof is to house as... ○ shoe is to sole / ⊗ bow is to boat
5. surgeon is to hospital as... ⊗ priest is to church / ○ teacher is to student
6. swim is to pool as... ⊗ read is to library / ○ javelin is to discus
7. lawyer is to client as... ○ doctor is to hospital / ⊗ banker is to depositor
8. falter is to hesitate as... ⊗ exact is to accurate / ○ passage is to passive
9. ornate is to austere as... ○ divan is to davenport / ⊗ elegant is to inferior
10. lather is to foam as... ⊗ larceny is to theft / ○ prohibit is to permit

Page 9

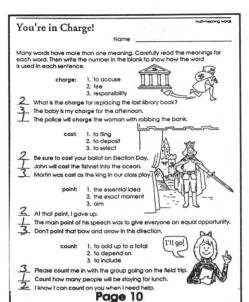

You're in Charge!

Many words have more than one meaning. Carefully read the meanings for each word. Then write the number in the blank to show how the word is used in each sentence.

charge: 1. to accuse 2. fee 3. responsibility

2 What is the charge for replacing the lost library book?
3 The baby is my charge for the afternoon.
1 The police will charge the woman with robbing the bank.

cast: 1. to fling 2. to deposit 3. to select

2 Be sure to cast your ballot on Election Day.
1 John will cast the fishnet into the ocean.
3 Martin was cast as the king in our class play.

point: 1. the essential idea 2. the exact moment 3. aim

2 At that point, I gave up.
1 The main point of his speech was to give everyone an equal opportunity.
3 Don't point that bow and arrow in this direction.

count: 1. to add up to a total 2. to depend on 3. to include

3 Please count me in with the group going on the field trip.
1 Count how many people will be staying for lunch.
2 I know I can count on you when I need help.

"I'll go!"

Page 10

The Space Race

Build a puzzle using the names of the United States' artificial satellites, spacecraft, and manned and unmanned orbiters. The letters already in the puzzle will help you.

STS (Space Transport System – the space shuttles)
ICE (International Cometary Explorer)
Magellan
LDEF (Long Range Exposure Facility)
Galileo
HST (Hubble Space Telescope)
Ulysses
GRO (Gamma Ray Orbiter)

Gemini
Apollo
Skylab
Pioneer
Viking

Explorer 1
Vanguard
Jupiter
Tiros
Echo
Freedom 7

Friendship 7
Telstar
Mariner
Faith 7
Ranger 7

Page 11

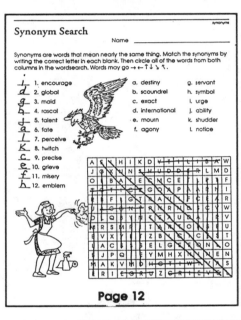

Synonym Search

Synonyms are words that mean nearly the same thing. Match the synonyms by writing the correct letter in each blank. Then circle all of the words from both columns in the wordsearch. Words may go → ↓ ↘ ↑ ↓ ↖

d 1. encourage
g 2. global
j 3. maid
b 4. rascal
a 5. talent
d 6. fate
i 7. perceive
k 8. twitch
c 9. precise
e 10. grieve
f 11. misery
h 12. emblem

a. destiny
b. scoundrel
c. exact
d. international
e. mourn
f. agony
g. servant
h. symbol
i. urge
j. ability
k. shudder
l. notice

Page 12

All Eyes on -ize!

The suffix -ize, which comes from the Greek suffix -izen, has several different meanings: to cause to be, to become like, to combine with, and to engage in. Complete each sentence below with the correct word from the Word Box.

Word Box

criticize	sterilize	colonize	categorize
idolize	specialize	italicize	realize
victimize	generalize	glamorize	tenderize

1. The dentist will **sterilize** the instruments.
2. The students needed to **categorize** the list of words.
3. **Italicize** every ship's name.
4. Some people **idolize** Elvis Presley.
5. A criminal will **victimize** people.
6. I'll **tenderize** the meat before roasting it.
7. A medical student can **specialize** in pediatrics.
8. Do you **realize** how fortunate you are?
9. This magazine always tries to **glamorize** women.
10. Be specific – don't **generalize** in your report.
11. People from Europe came to **colonize** the New World.
12. I wish you wouldn't be so quick to **criticize** me.

Page 13

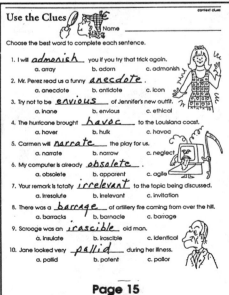

This Is Duck Soup!

An idiom is a phrase or expression that has a different meaning from its literal definition. For example, something that is 'duck soup' is easily accomplished. Rewrite each sentence using a word or phrase from the Word Box to replace each bold-faced idiom.

Word Box

| deferred | excited | an exaggerator | break | agree |
| depressed | disbelieve | get angry | clumsy | help |

1. I've never seen Jamal so down in the mouth.
   I've never seen Jamal so depressed.
2. I put no stock in Mr. Smith's claim of being the richest man in town.
   I disbelieve Mr. Smith's claim of being the richest man in town.
3. My proposal was put on ice until the next meeting.
   My proposal was deferred until the next meeting.
4. Now, don't fly off the handle just because I won't go.
   Now, don't get angry just because I won't go.
5. Steven is all wound up about Halloween.
   Steven is excited about Halloween.
6. Claude and I don't see eye to eye on this point.
   Claude and I don't agree on this point.
7. Please lend a hand – this trunk is heavy.
   Please help – this trunk is heavy.
8. No one believes Carla because she's full of hot air.
   No one believes Carla because she's an exaggerator.
9. The teacher said to take five before resuming the test.
   The teacher said to break before resuming the test.
10. Don't take Paul shopping – he's a bull in a china closet!
    Don't take Paul shopping – he's clumsy.

Page 14

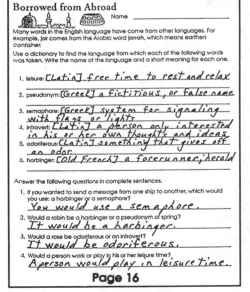

Use the Clues

Choose the best word to complete each sentence.

1. I will **admonish** you if you try that trick again.
   a. array b. adorn c. admonish
2. Mr. Perez read us a funny **anecdote**.
   a. anecdote b. antidote c. icon
3. Try not to be **envious** of Jennifer's new outfit.
   a. inane b. envious c. ethical
4. The hurricane brought **havoc** to the Louisiana coast.
   a. hover b. hulk c. havoc
5. Carmen will **narrate** the play for us.
   a. narrate b. narrow c. neglect
6. My computer is already **obsolete**.
   a. obsolete b. apparent c. agile
7. Your remark is totally **irrelevant** to the topic being discussed.
   a. irresolute b. irrelevant c. invitation
8. There was a **barrage** of artillery fire coming from over the hill.
   a. barracks b. barnacle c. barrage
9. Scrooge was an **irascible** old man.
   a. insulate b. irascible c. identical
10. Jane looked very **pallid** during her illness.
    a. pallid b. patent c. pallor

Page 15

Borrowed from Abroad

Many words in the English language have come from other languages. For example, jar comes from the Arabic word jarrah, which means earthen container.

Use a dictionary to find the language from which each of the following words was taken. Write the name of the language and a short meaning for each one.

1. leisure: [Latin] free time to rest and relax
2. pseudonym: [Greek] a fictitious, or false name
3. semaphore: [Greek] system for signaling with flags or lights
4. introvert: [Latin] a person only interested in his or her own thoughts and ideas
5. odoriferous: [Latin] something that gives off an odor
6. harbinger: [Old French] a forerunner, herald

Answer the following questions in complete sentences.

1. If you wanted to send a message from one ship to another, which would you use: a harbinger or a semaphore?
   You would use a semaphore.
2. Would a robin be a harbinger or a pseudonym of spring?
   It would be a harbinger.
3. Would a rose be odoriferous or an introvert?
   It would be odoriferous.
4. Would a person work or play in his or her leisure time?
   A person would play in leisure time.

Page 16

Star Light, Star Bright

Name _____

The twenty brightest stars are listed in order of their brightness. Circle their names in the wordsearch. Words may go → ← ↓ ↑ ↘ ↙.

Word Box

Sirius	Procyon	Spica
Canopus	Betelgeuse	Antares
Alpha Centauri	Achernar	Pollux
Arcturus	Beta Centauri	Fomalhaut
Vega	Altair	Deneb
Capella	Alpha Crucis	Beta Crucis
Rigel	Aldebaran	

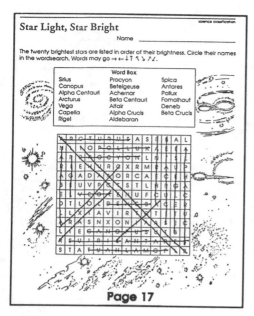

Page 17

Produce the Produce

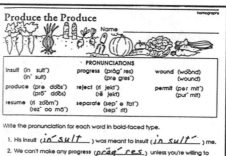

Name _____

PRONUNCIATIONS

insult (in´ sult´)
(in´ sult)

progress (präg´ res)
(pre gres´)

wound (woond)
(wound)

produce (pre doos´)
(prō´ doos)

reject (ri jekt´)
(rē´ jekt)

permit (per mit´)
(pur´ mit)

resume (ri zoom´)
(rez´ oo mā´)

separate (sep´ e rat´)
(sep´ rit)

Write the pronunciation for each word in bold-faced type.

1. His insult (in sult) was meant to insult (in sult´) me.

2. We can't make any progress (präg´ res) unless you're willing to progress (pre gres´) to the next step.

3. The nurse wound (wound) the bandage around the wound (woond).

4. Did the farmer produce (pre doos´) all of that produce (prō´ doos) on his farm?

5. He might reject (rē´ jekt) any ideas of what to do with the reject (ri jekt´).

6. The police will permit (per mit´) you to park here if you have a valid permit (pur´ mit).

7. You can resume (ri zoom´) writing your resume (rez´ oo mā´).

8. Please separate (sep´ e rat´) the laundry into two separate (sep´ rit) loads.

Page 18

Weird Words

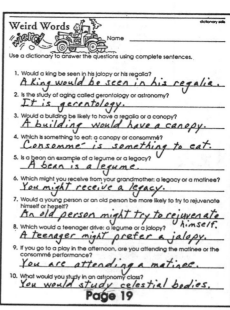

Name _____

Use a dictionary to answer the questions using complete sentences.

1. Would a king be seen in his jalopy or his regalia?
   A king would be seen in his regalia.

2. Is the study of aging called gerontology or astronomy?
   It is gerontology.

3. Would a building be likely to have a regalia or a canopy?
   A building would have a canopy.

4. Which is something to eat: a canopy or consommé?
   Consommé is something to eat.

5. Is a bean an example of a legume or a legacy?
   A bean is a legume.

6. Which might you receive from your grandmother: a legacy or a matinee?
   You might receive a legacy.

7. Would a young person or an old person be more likely to try to rejuvenate himself or herself?
   An old person might try to rejuvenate himself.

8. Which would a teenager drive: a legume or a jalopy?
   A teenager might prefer a jalopy.

9. If you go to a play in the afternoon, are you attending the matinee or the consommé performance?
   You are attending a matinee.

10. What would you study in an astronomy class?
    You would study celestial bodies.

Page 19

Crossword Careers

Name _____

Build a puzzle with the career names in the Word Box. Hint: Build off electrician.

Word Box

engineer	judge	nurse	pilot	artist	mechanic
banker	lawyer	singer	chemist	dentist	architect
plumber	teacher	clerk	author	painter	astronaut

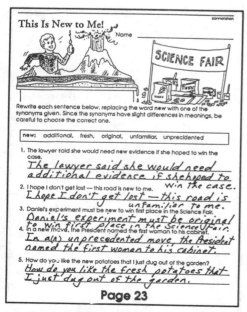

Page 20

You're Too Smart for Me!

Name _____

Many words have more than one meaning. Carefully read the meanings for each word. Then write the number in the blank to show how the word is used in each sentence.

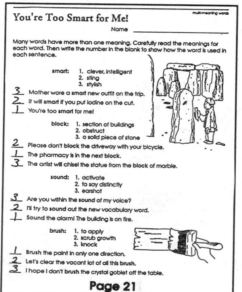

smart: 1. clever, intelligent
        2. sting
        3. stylish

3 Mother wore a smart new outfit on the trip.
2 It will smart if you put iodine on the cut.
1 You're too smart for me!

block: 1. section of buildings
        2. obstruct
        3. a solid piece of stone

2 Please don't block the driveway with your bicycle.
1 The pharmacy is in the next block.
3 The artist will chisel the statue from the block of marble.

sound: 1. activate
        2. to say distinctly
        3. earshot

3 Are you within the sound of my voice?
2 I'll try to sound out the new vocabulary word.
1 Sound the alarm! The building is on fire.

brush: 1. to apply
        2. scrub growth
        3. knock

1 Brush the paint in only one direction.
2 Let's clear the vacant lot of all this brush.
3 I hope I don't brush the crystal goblet off the table.

Page 21

It's All Greek to Me!

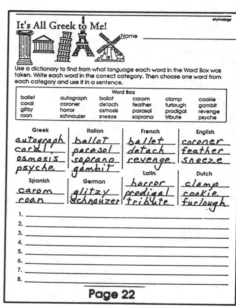

Name _____

Use a dictionary to find from what language each word in the Word Box was taken. Write each word in the correct category. Then choose one word from each category and use it in a sentence.

Word Box

ballet	autograph	ballot	carom	clamp	cookie
coral	coroner	detach	feather	furlough	gambit
glitzy	horror	osmosis	parasol	prodigal	revenge
roan	schnauzer	sneeze	soprano	tribute	psyche

Greek	Italian	French	English
autograph	ballot	ballet	coroner
coral	parasol	detach	feather
osmosis	soprano	revenge	sneeze
psyche	gambit		

Spanish	German	Latin	Dutch
carom	glitzy	horror	clamp
roan	schnauzer	prodigal	cookie
		tribute	furlough

1. _____
2. _____
3. _____
4. _____
5. _____
6. _____
7. _____
8. _____

Page 22

This Is New to Me!

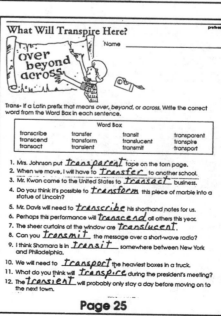

Name _____

Rewrite each sentence below, replacing the word new with one of the synonyms given. Since the synonyms have slight differences in meanings, be careful to choose the correct one.

new: additional, fresh, original, unfamiliar, unprecedented

1. The lawyer said she would need new evidence if she hoped to win the case.
   The lawyer said she would need additional evidence if she hoped to win the case.

2. I hope I don't get lost — this road is new to me.
   I hope I don't get lost — this road is unfamiliar to me.

3. Daniel's experiment must be new to win first place in the Science Fair.
   Daniel's experiment must be original to win first place in the Science Fair.

4. In a new move, the President named the first woman to his cabinet.
   In a(n) unprecedented move, the President named the first woman to his cabinet.

5. How do you like the new potatoes that I just dug out of the garden?
   How do you like the fresh potatoes that I just dug out of the garden?

Page 23

Get in Shape!

Name _____

Use the code to write a synonym for each word. Follow the example.

Example: say – ⌐∩⌐⌐   tell

t	p	a
s	e	l

1. flavor – ⌐∟⌐∩   taste
2. decline – ⌐∟∪∩   lapse
3. overtake – ∪∟⌐⌐   pass
4. pilfer – ⌐∩∟⌐   steal
5. satisfy – ∟∪∪∩∟∩   appease
6. fewest – ⌐∩∟⌐⌐   least
7. strike – ⌐∟∪   slap
8. spaghetti – ∪∟⌐∪⌐   pasta
9. tardy – ⌐∟∩∩   late
10. fold – ∪∩∩∟⌐   pleat
11. favorite – ∪∩⌐   pet
12. hide – ∪∩⌐⌐   pelt
13. skin – ∪∩∩⌐   peel
14. final – ⌐∟⌐⌐   last
15. rap – ⌐∟∪   tap
16. ring – ∪∩∟⌐   peal
17. former – ∪∟⌐⌐   past
18. relieve – ∩∟⌐∩   ease
19. ingest – ∩∟⌐   eat
20. chair – ⌐∩∟∪   seat
21. spirit – ∪∩∪   pep
22. jump – ⌐∩∟∪   leap

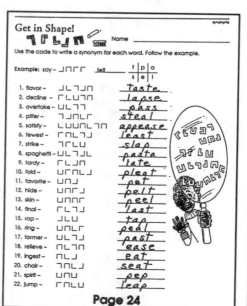

Page 24

What Will Transpire Here?

over
beyond
across

Name _____

Trans- is a Latin prefix that means over, beyond, or across. Write the correct word from the Word Box in each sentence.

Word Box

transcribe	transfer	transit	transparent
transcend	transform	translucent	transpire
transact	transient	transmit	transport

1. Mrs. Johnson put *transparent* tape on the torn page.
2. When we move, I will have to *transfer* to another school.
3. Mr. Kwan came to the United States to *transact* business.
4. Do you think it's possible to *transform* this piece of marble into a statue of Lincoln?
5. Mr. Davis will need to *transcribe* his shorthand notes for us.
6. Perhaps this performance will *transcend* all others this year.
7. The sheer curtains at the window are *translucent*.
8. Can you *transmit* the message over a short-wave radio?
9. I think Shamara is in *transit* somewhere between New York and Philadelphia.
10. We will need to *transport* the heaviest boxes in a truck.
11. What do you think will *transpire* during the president's meeting?
12. The *transient* will probably only stay a day before moving on to the next town.

Page 25

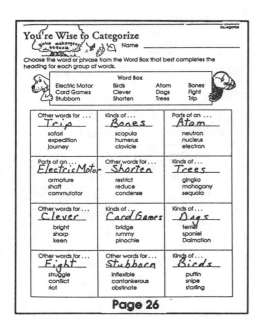

You're Wise to Categorize

Name _____

Choose the word or phrase from the Word Box that best completes the heading for each group of words.

Word Box
Electric Motor, Birds, Atom, Bones, Card Games, Clever, Dogs, Fight, Stubborn, Shorten, Trees, Trip

Other words for ... **Trip**	Kinds of ... **Bones**	Parts of an ... **Atom**
safari	scapula	neutron
expedition	humerus	nucleus
journey	clavicle	electron

Parts of an ... **Electric Motor**	Other words for ... **Shorten**	Kinds of ... **Trees**
armature	restrict	gingko
shaft	reduce	mahogany
commutator	condense	sequoia

Other words for ... **Clever**	Kinds of ... **Card Games**	Kinds of ... **Dogs**
bright	bridge	terrier
sharp	rummy	spaniel
keen	pinochle	Dalmation

Other words for ... **Fight**	Other words for ... **Stubborn**	Kinds of ... **Birds**
struggle	inflexible	puffin
conflict	cantankerous	snipe
riot	obstinate	starling

Page 26

You're a Pro!

Name _____

The Latin prefix pro- has several meanings: *moving forward, substituting for,* and *supporting.* Match each word with its meaning by writing the correct letter in the blank.

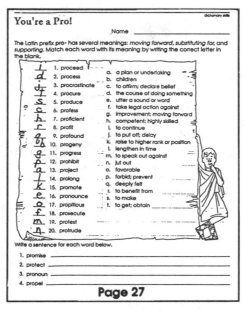

1. proceed — l
2. process — d
3. procrastinate — i
4. procure — t
5. produce — s
6. profess — c
7. proficient — h
8. profit — r
9. profound — q
10. progeny — b
11. progress — g
12. prohibit — p
13. project — a
14. prolong — j
15. promote — k
16. pronounce — e
17. propitious — o
18. prosecute — f
19. protest — m
20. protrude — n

a. a plan or undertaking
b. children
c. to affirm; declare belief
d. the course of doing something
e. utter a sound or word
f. take legal action against
g. improvement; moving forward
h. competent; highly skilled
i. to put off; delay
j. lengthen in time
k. raise to higher rank or position
l. to continue
m. to speak out against
n. jut out
o. favorable
p. forbid; prevent
q. deeply felt
r. to benefit from
s. to make
t. to get; obtain

Write a sentence for each word below.

1. promise _____
2. protect _____
3. pronoun _____
4. propel _____

Page 27

Make No Bones About It

Name _____

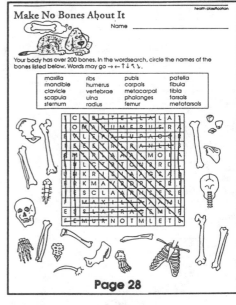

Your body has over 200 bones. In the wordsearch, circle the names of the bones listed below. Words may go → ← ↑ ↓ ↘ ↙.

maxilla, mandible, clavicle, scapula, sternum, ribs, humerus, vertebrae, ulna, radius, pubis, carpals, metacarpal, phalanges, femur, patella, fibula, tarsals, metatarsals

Page 28

Out of Sight!

Name _____

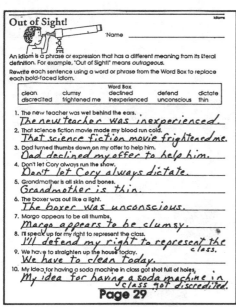

An idiom is a phrase or expression that has a different meaning from its literal definition. For example, "Out of Sight!" means *outrageous.*

Rewrite each sentence using a word or phrase from the Word Box to replace each bold-faced idiom.

Word Box
clean, clumsy, declined, defend, dictate, discredited, frightened me, inexperienced, unconscious, thin

1. The new teacher was wet behind the ears.
The new teacher was inexperienced.
2. That science fiction movie made my blood run cold.
That science fiction movie frightened me.
3. Dad turned thumbs down on my offer to help him.
Dad declined my offer to help him.
4. Don't let Cory always run the show.
Don't let Cory always dictate.
5. Grandmother is all skin and bones.
Grandmother is thin.
6. The boxer was out like a light.
The boxer was unconscious.
7. Margo appears to be all thumbs.
Margo appears to be clumsy.
8. I'll speak up for my right to represent the class.
I'll defend my right to represent the class.
9. We have to straighten up the house today.
We have to clean today.
10. My idea for having a soda machine in class got shot full of holes.
My idea for having a soda machine in class got discredited.

Page 29

Similar in Some Way

Name _____

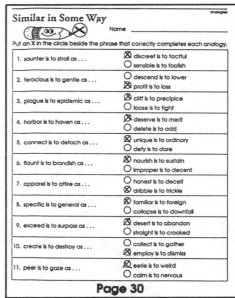

Put an X in the circle beside the phrase that correctly completes each analogy.

1. saunter is to stroll as ...
   ☒ discreet is to tactful
   ○ sensible is to foolish
2. ferocious is to gentle as ...
   ○ descend is to lower
   ☒ profit is to loss
3. plague is to epidemic as ...
   ☒ cliff is to precipice
   ○ loose is to tight
4. harbor is to haven as ...
   ☒ deserve is to merit
   ○ delete is to add
5. connect is to detach as ...
   ☒ unique is to ordinary
   ○ defy is to dare
6. flaunt is to brandish as ...
   ☒ nourish is to sustain
   ○ improper is to decent
7. apparel is to attire as ...
   ○ honest is to deceit
   ☒ dribble is to trickle
8. specific is to general as ...
   ☒ familiar is to foreign
   ○ collapse is to downfall
9. exceed is to surpass as ...
   ☒ desert is to abandon
   ○ straight is to crooked
10. create is to destroy as ...
   ○ collect is to gather
   ☒ employ is to dismiss
11. peer is to gaze as ...
   ☒ eerie is to weird
   ○ calm is to nervous

Page 30

Don't Get in a Stew Over This

Name _____

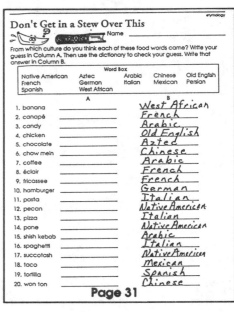

From which culture do you think each of these food words came? Write your guess in Column A. Then use the dictionary to check your guess. Write that answer in Column B.

Word Box
Native American, Aztec, Arabic, Chinese, Old English, French, Spanish, German, Italian, Mexican, Persian, West African

	A	B
1. banana		West African
2. canapé		French
3. candy		Arabic
4. chicken		Old English
5. chocolate		Aztec
6. chow mein		Chinese
7. coffee		Arabic
8. éclair		French
9. fricassee		French
10. hamburger		German
11. pasta		Italian
12. pecan		Native American
13. pizza		Italian
14. pone		Native American
15. shish kebab		Arabic
16. spaghetti		Italian
17. succotash		Native American
18. taco		Mexican
19. tortilla		Spanish
20. won ton		Chinese

Page 31

Simply Synonyms

Name _____

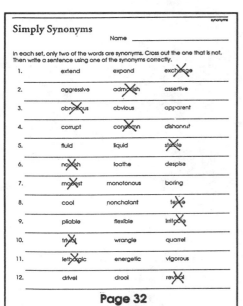

In each set, only two of the words are synonyms. Cross out the one that is not. Then write a sentence using one of the synonyms correctly.

1. extend — expand — ~~exchange~~
2. aggressive — ~~admonish~~ — assertive
3. ~~obnoxious~~ — obvious — apparent
4. corrupt — ~~condemn~~ — dishonest
5. fluid — liquid — ~~stable~~
6. ~~nourish~~ — loathe — despise
7. ~~modest~~ — monotonous — boring
8. cool — nonchalant — ~~tense~~
9. pliable — flexible — ~~irritable~~
10. ~~trivial~~ — wrangle — quarrel
11. ~~lethargic~~ — energetic — vigorous
12. drivel — drool — ~~revel~~

Page 32

This Is So Fine

Name _____

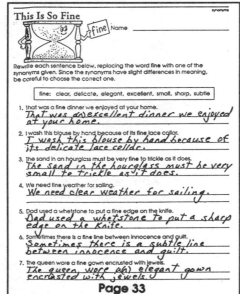

Rewrite each sentence below, replacing the word fine with one of the synonyms given. Since the synonyms have slight differences in meaning, be careful to choose the correct one.

fine: clear, delicate, elegant, excellent, small, sharp, subtle

1. That was a fine dinner we enjoyed at your home.
That was an excellent dinner we enjoyed at your home.
2. I wash this blouse by hand because of its fine lace collar.
I wash this blouse by hand because of its delicate lace collar.
3. The sand in an hourglass must be very fine to trickle as it does.
The sand in the hourglass must be very small to trickle as it does.
4. We need fine weather for sailing.
We need clear weather for sailing.
5. Dad used a whetstone to put a fine edge on the knife.
Dad used a whetstone to put a sharp edge on the knife.
6. Sometimes there is a fine line between innocence and guilt.
Sometimes there is a subtle line between innocence and guilt.
7. The queen wore a fine gown encrusted with jewels.
The queen wore an elegant gown encrusted with jewels.

Page 33

Are You in Your Element?

Name _____

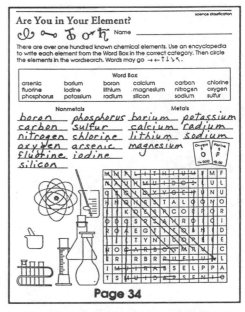

There are over one hundred known chemical elements. Use an encyclopedia to write each element from the Word Box in the correct category. Then circle the elements in the wordsearch. Words may go → ← ↑ ↓ ↘ ↙.

Word Box
arsenic, barium, boron, calcium, carbon, chlorine, fluorine, iodine, lithium, magnesium, nitrogen, oxygen, phosphorus, potassium, radium, silicon, sodium, sulfur

Nonmetals
boron, phosphorus, carbon, sulfur, nitrogen, chlorine, oxygen, arsenic, fluorine, iodine, silicon

Metals
barium, potassium, calcium, radium, lithium, sodium, magnesium

Page 34

Page 35 — Quite a (Feat, Feet)!

homophones

Name _____

Circle the correct homophones in each sentence.

1. It was quite a (feat, feet) to jump 18 (feat, feet) in the long jump.
2. The mayor went before the (council, counsel) to (council, counsel) them about the new laws.
3. I will (ascent, assent) to try the (ascent, assent) of Mount Everest.
4. How can you be so (callous, callus) about my painful (callous, callus)?
5. You are sure to receive a (complement, compliment) if you (complement, compliment) that piece of pie with a scoop of ice cream.
6. There is a (roomer, rumor) that the new (roomer, rumor) at the boardinghouse is from China.
7. The liquid in that (vial, vile) tastes (vial, vile) to me.
8. Can you imagine what would (cause, caws) the crow's loud (cause, caws)?
9. On what do you (base, bass) your opinion that the (base, bass) is the best instrument?
10. The knight admitted his (gilt, guilt) of taking the sword covered with (gilt, guilt).

On the lines below, write a sentence for each pair of homophones.

not, knot _____

main, mane _____

mall, male _____

weak, week _____

sighs, size _____

Page 36 — Title Time

categorize

Name _____

Choose the word or phrase from the Word Box that best completes the heading for each group of words.

Word Box
Cell · Dances · Eye · Fierce · Flower · Gems · Red · Shapes · Speech · Teeth · Weird · Sporting Events

Places for... **Sporting Events**	Names of... **Teeth**	Parts of a **Flower**
arena	bicuspid	pistil
natatorium	molar	stamen
coliseum	incisor	sepal

Parts of a **Cell**	Kinds of... **Shapes**	Other words for... **Weird**
nucleus	trapezoid	uncanny
cytoplasm	octagon	peculiar
chloroplasts	parallelogram	strange

Kinds of... **Gems**	Parts of **Speech**	Shades of... **Red**
opal	conjunction	vermilion
topaz	participle	crimson
peridot	preposition	scarlet

Words for... **Fierce**	Kinds of... **Dances**	Parts of the... **Eye**
feral	jig	cornea
bestial	minuet	lens
vicious	bolero	retina

Page 37 — The Subject Is Homograph

homographs

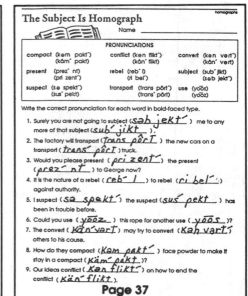

Name _____

PRONUNCIATIONS

compact (kem pakt´) (käm´ pakt)	conflict (ken flikt´) (kän´ flikt)	convert (ken vert´) (kän´ vert)
present (prez´ nt) (pri zent´)	rebel (reb´ l) (ri bel´)	subject (sub´ jikt) (sab jekt´)
suspect (sə spekt´) (sus´ pekt)	transport (trans pôrt´) (trans´ pôrt)	use (yo͞oz) (yo͞os)

Write the correct pronunciation for each word in bold-faced type.

1. Surely you are not going to subject (_sab jekt´_) me to any more of that subject (_sub´ jikt_).
2. The factory will transport (_trans pôrt_) the new cars on a transport (_trans´ pôrt_) truck.
3. Would you please present (_pri zent´_) the present (_prez´ nt_) to George now?
4. It is the nature of a rebel (_reb´ l_) to rebel (_ri bel´_) against authority.
5. I suspect (_sə spekt´_) the suspect (_sus´ pekt_) has been in trouble before.
6. Could you use (_yo͞oz_) this rope for another use (_yo͞os_)?
7. The convert (_kän´ vart_) may try to convert (_kah vart´_) others to his cause.
8. How do they compact (_kəm pakt´_) face powder to make it stay in a compact (_käm´ pakt_)?
9. Our ideas conflict (_kən flikt´_) on how to end the conflict (_kän´ flikt_).

Page 38 — Analyze These Analogies

analogies

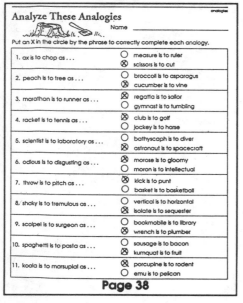

Name _____

Put an X in the circle by the phrase to correctly complete each analogy.

1. ax is to chop as...
   ○ measure is to ruler
   ⊗ scissors is to cut
2. peach is to tree as...
   ○ broccoli is to asparagus
   ⊗ cucumber is to vine
3. marathon is to runner as...
   ⊗ regatta is to sailor
   ○ gymnast is to tumbling
4. racket is to tennis as...
   ⊗ club is to golf
   ○ jockey is to horse
5. scientist is to laboratory as...
   ○ bathyscaph is to diver
   ⊗ astronaut is to spacecraft
6. odious is to disgusting as...
   ⊗ morose is to gloomy
   ○ moron is to intellectual
7. throw is to pitch as...
   ⊗ kick is to punt
   ○ basket is to basketball
8. shaky is to tremulous as...
   ⊗ vertical is to horizontal
   ○ isolate is to sequester
9. scalpel is to surgeon as...
   ○ bookmobile is to library
   ⊗ wrench is to plumber
10. spaghetti is to pasta as...
    ○ sausage is to bacon
    ⊗ kumquat is to fruit
11. koala is to marsupial as...
    ⊗ porcupine is to rodent
    ○ emu is to pelican

Page 39 — Watch Out!

dictionary skills

Name _____

Match the correct definition to each word beginning with out-.

_e_ 1. outage — a. a rejected person
_p_ 2. outback — b. clothes worn together
_h_ 3. outbid — c. market for specific goods
_q_ 4. outboard — d. amount produced
_j_ 5. outbreak — e. accidental loss of electric power
_a_ 6. outburst — f. result
_v_ 7. outcast — g. no longer fashionable
_u_ 8. outclass — h. to offer more
_f_ 9. outcome — i. sudden release of emotion
_r_ 10. outcry — j. playing area beyond infield
_x_ 11. outdoors — k. criminal
_K_ 12. outfield — l. viewpoint
_b_ 13. outfit — m. extremely violent act
_l_ 14. outlaw — n. straightforward
_s_ 15. outlay — o. Australia's wild inland region
_c_ 16. outlet — p. outside the boat
_w_ 17. outlive — q. strong protest
_m_ 18. outlook — r. money spent
_g_ 19. outmoded — s. base away from home
_t_ 20. outpost — t. sudden occurence
_n_ 21. outraged — u. to surpass
_d_ 22. outrage — v. endure longer than
_i_ 23. outreach — w. in the open
_o_ 24. outright — x.

Page 40 — What's in a Name?

etymology

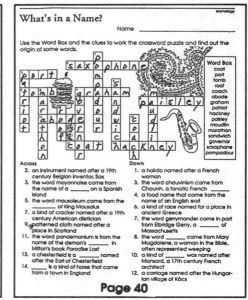

Name _____

Use the Word Box and the clues to work the crossword puzzle and find out the origin of some words.

Word Box
coat · port · tomb · roof · coach · graham · patriot · hackney · paisley · maudlin · marathon · sandwich · governor · saxophone · pompadour

Across
2. an instrument named after a 19th century Belgian inventor, Sax
3. the word mayonnaise came from the name of a _____ on a Spanish island
5. the word mausoleum came from the _____ of King Mausolus
7. a kind of cracker named after a 19th century American dietician
9. patterned cloth named after a place in Scotland
11. the word pandemonium is from the name of the demon's _____ in Milton's book *Paradise Lost*
13. a chesterfield is a _____ named after the Earl of Chesterfield
14. _____ is a kind of horse that came from a town in England

Down
1. a hairdo named after a French woman
3. the word chauvinism came from Chauvin, a fanatic French _____
4. a food name that came from the name of an English earl
6. a kind of race named for a place in ancient Greece
7. the word gerrymander came in part from Eldridge Gerry, a _____ of Massachusetts
8. the word _____ came from Mary Magdalene, a woman in the Bible, often represented weeping
10. a kind of _____ was named after Mansard, a 17th century French architect
12. a carriage named after the Hungarian village of Kócs

Page 41 — Crackerjack Word Find

digraphs

Name _____

Circle all the words containing the ck digraph in the wordsearch.

Word Box
sack · track · snack · racket · bracket
back · slick · brick · hockey · backward
lock · slack · stack · cackle · crackpot
lick · smack · socks · beckon · sprocket
luck · stock · crack · jockey · necklace
pack · speck · tacks · pocket · bareback
peck · wreck · stick · jacket · checkers
tuck · pluck · black · attack · cockroach
lack · clock · rocket · cracker · woodpecker
hack · rocky · locket · crackle · crackerjack
rack

Page 42 — Explore Context Clues

context clues

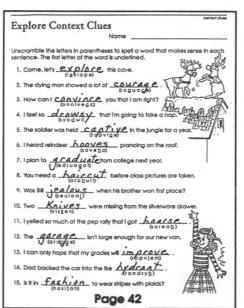

Name _____

Unscramble the letters in parentheses to spell a word that makes sense in each sentence. The first letter of the word is underlined.

1. Come, let's _explore_ (xplroe) this cave.
2. The dying man showed a lot of _courage_ (rogauce).
3. How can I _convince_ (onnivce) you that I am right?
4. I feel so _drowsy_ (sydowr) that I'm going to take a nap.
5. The soldier was held _captive_ (tapvice) in the jungle for a year.
6. I heard reindeer _hooves_ (soveh) prancing on the roof.
7. I plan to _graduate_ from college next year. (druagat)
8. You need a _haircut_ (archuit) before class pictures are taken.
9. Was Bill _jealous_ (seuloaj) when his brother won first place?
10. Two _knives_ (visken) were missing from the silverware drawer.
11. I yelled so much at the pep rally that I got _hoarse_ (soreah).
12. The _garage_ (aradge) isn't large enough for our new van.
13. I can only hope that my grades will _improve_ (rpovlem).
14. Dad backed the car into the fire _hydrant_ (tandryh).
15. Is it in _fashion_ (nosifah) to wear stripes with plaids?

Page 43 — Antonym Action

antonyms

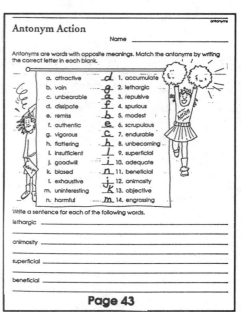

Name _____

Antonyms are words with opposite meanings. Match the antonyms by writing the correct letter in each blank.

a. attractive   _d_ 1. accumulate
b. vain   _g_ 2. lethargic
c. unbearable   _a_ 3. repulsive
d. dissipate   _f_ 4. spurious
e. remiss   _b_ 5. modest
f. authentic   _e_ 6. scrupulous
g. vigorous   _c_ 7. endurable
h. flattering   _h_ 8. unbecoming
i. insufficient   _l_ 9. superficial
j. goodwill   _i_ 10. adequate
k. biased   _n_ 11. beneficial
l. exhaustive   _j_ 12. animosity
m. uninteresting   _k_ 13. objective
n. harmful   _m_ 14. engrossing

Write a sentence for each of the following words.

lethargic _____

animosity _____

superficial _____

beneficial _____